D1290670

So many people talk about the Bible, but so few have actually read it. This new, accessible version bridges that gap. It provides clear insight into the Bible's main themes, figures, and events from Creation to Revelation in under two hours. The *100-Minute Bible* is a convenient and enlightening way of experiencing the greatest story ever told.

Michael Hinton was born in Bristol, England. He was a school headmaster before becoming an Anglican minister for a village parish in Kent, and has written several books. He unveiled *The 100-Minute Bible* at Canterbury Cathedral in 2005.

THE
100-MINUTE BIBLE

This edition published in the United States and Canada in 2007
by Chronicle Books LLC
First published in the United Kingdom in 2005,
by The 100-Minute Press, Canterbury, England
Copyright © 2005 by The 100-Minute Press

The use of short portions of this publication, i.e., up to one
section, is permitted without reference to the publisher. The
publisher requests that the origin of such extracts should
be acknowledged as *The 100-Minute Bible*.

Library of Congress Cataloging-in-Publication
Data is available.

ISBN-10: 0-8118-5621-8
ISBN-13: 978-0-8118-5621-8

Manufactured in Canada

Designed by Studio Moze
Typeset in Gotham 8/13 and Bauer Bodoni 9.5/13
Abridged by Michael Hinton
Map design by Arthur Mount

10 9 8 7 6 5 4 3 2 1

Chronicle Books LLC
680 Second Street
San Francisco, California 94107

www.chroniclebooks.com

THE
100-MINUTE BIBLE

Abridged by Michael Hinton

TABLE OF CONTENTS

Preface 8

1 In the Beginning 12

2 Abraham 14

3 Jacob and His Family 16

4 Moses 18

5 The Giving of the Law 20

6 Joshua and the Judges 22

7 Samuel, Saul, and David 26

8 David as King 28

9 The Psalms 30

10 Solomon and the Division of His Kingdom 32

11 Elijah and Elisha 34

12 The Northern Kingdom's Downfall; Isaiah 36

13 Jonah 38

14 The Southern Kingdom's Downfall; Jeremiah 40

15 Exile and Return 42

16 The Writings: Job and Ecclesiastes 44

17 The Centuries Before the Coming of Jesus 46

18 The Visions of Zechariah and Mary 48

19 Jesus Is Born 50

20 Jesus' Early Life 52

21 Jesus' Baptism and Temptations 54

22 Jesus Begins His Ministry 56

23 Jesus' Ministry Continues 60

24 Jesus Chooses the Twelve 62

25 The Sermon on the Mount 64

26 Teaching on Prayer 66

27 Parables 68

28 Jesus Answers Questions 70

29 Miracles of Healing 72

30 Raising the Dead 74

31 Nature Miracles 76

32 Who Is Jesus? 78

33 Jesus' True Nature 80

34 On the Way to Jerusalem 82

35 Arrival at Jerusalem 84

36 Jesus Teaches in the Temple 86

37 Teaching about Judgment 88

38 The Last Supper 90

39 The Garden of Gethsemane 92

40 The Trials of Jesus 94

41 The Crucifixion 96

42 Jesus Rises from the Dead 98

43 Further Resurrection Appearances 100

44 The Ascension, Pentecost, and the Early Church 102

45 The Christian Church Grows and Develops 104

46 Further Expansion: Paul's Travels 108

47 The Young Church: Doctrine 110

48 The Young Church: Difficulties 112

49 The Young Church: Daily Life 114

50 Revelation 116

PREFACE

The Bible must be the most popular yet least-read book in the world! It looks so complex, so long, and is in a language from a previous era. And yet it's the greatest story ever told, the ultimate love story, the biography of God himself.

It is quite true that the Bible is complex. It was written over sixteen centuries, in sixty-six books, and by scores of different writers, each of whom has their own style. *The 100-Minute Bible* is designed for people who may not know very much about the Christian faith but want to know why the Bible is so popular with two billion Christians around the world. It's for people who want an easy access into the central Christian story. This little book represents a first-class way of doing just that. It's clear, succinct, an easy read—yet is still comprehensive. A word of warning, though! Do not be put off by the bloodthirstiness of the first few sections—this is the social context into which God sends his own son to show a new way of living.

The 100-Minute Bible is also for Christians who want to revisit the big picture. Read this and you'll see the whole sweep of God's loving purposes for his world and all its people.

Unlike the traditional Bible, three-quarters of which is devoted to the centuries before Christ, this version centers on Christ's life and impact on society. This is simply because the key to unlocking the Bible is Jesus Christ. It's as if he is the great explosion that happened in the center of history and the Bible is a record of its impact.

If we're to understand Christianity more fully, ultimately we'll need to understand something of the context in which it was written, the text itself, and what it meant to those who first read it. But first we need to get hold of the overall story. And this is what *The 100-Minute Bible* provides so succinctly and elegantly.

Bishop John Pritchard
Oxford, England

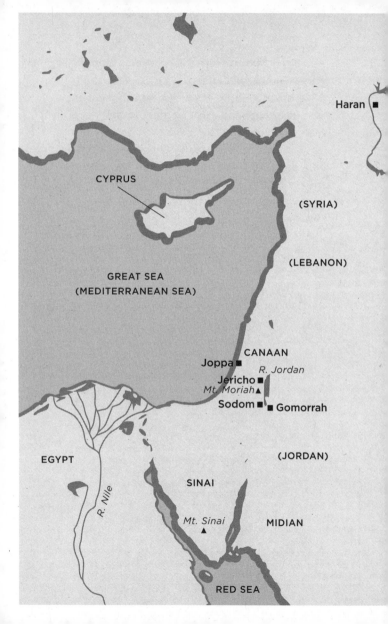

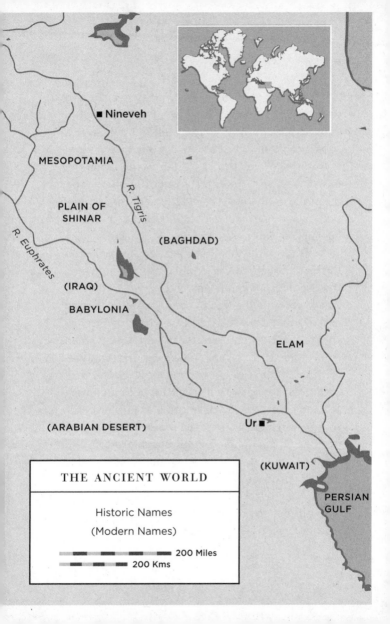

1 IN THE BEGINNING

In the beginning God created heaven and earth over a period of six days. First he created light and darkness; then the vault of the heavens, separating the water above from the water below; then the dry land and all that grows in it. On the fourth day God created the sun, the moon, and the stars; on the fifth the creatures of the sea and sky; and on the sixth those of the land, including humankind. On the seventh day God rested.

God made the first man, Adam, from the dust, and breathed life into him. He placed him in the beautiful and fertile garden of Eden, forbidding him to eat from the tree of the knowledge of good and evil that grew there. Because he thought man should not be alone, he created the first woman from Adam's rib; Adam named her Eve. Eve was tempted by the serpent, the most cunning of creatures; she took fruit from the forbidden tree, ate some herself, and gave some to her husband. As a punishment, God expelled them both from the garden; he condemned men to arduous toil, and women to pain in childbearing and to submission to their husbands.

Adam and Eve bore two sons: Cain, who worked the land, and Abel, who cared for sheep. God favored Abel's offerings over those of Cain.

Cain was angry and murdered Abel; as a punishment God sentenced him to become a wanderer forever. Adam and Eve had further children, and so the human race spread and multiplied.

In subsequent generations humankind's wickedness became more and more apparent, and God decided a fresh start was necessary. He chose Noah, the only blameless man of the time, and told him to build a boat in which he could shelter his family and living creatures of every kind. Then God sent a flood that destroyed every other living thing. When the flood receded, God sent the rainbow as a sign that he would never destroy his creation again.

After the world was repopulated, there was a time when everyone spoke the same language. People migrated to the fertile plain of Shinar between the rivers Tigris and Euphrates; there they decided to build a city named Babel, and a tower that would reach right up to heaven. To thwart them, God confused their language so that they could not understand each other, and scattered them all over the earth.

Genesis 1–11

2 ABRAHAM

Many generations later a man named Abram lived in Ur of the Chaldees. His family moved to Haran; then, at God's command, he journeyed south and led a nomadic life until, by agreement with his kinsman Lot, he settled on the west side of the river Jordan. Lot settled in the valley of the Jordan itself, in the city of Sodom. When fire from heaven fell on Sodom and the nearby city of Gomorrah as a punishment for their wickedness, God's intervention ensured that Lot was spared.

In due course God made a covenant (a binding agreement) with Abram, promising him a son, descendants as many as the stars in the sky in number, and possession of the whole land of Canaan. As a sign of the covenant, God renamed Abram Abraham (which means "father of a multitude"), and he and all the males of his family were circumcised. By now he was a man of great wealth in cattle, silver, and gold, but he and his wife were childless.

In their extreme old age, and by a special providence from God, Abraham and his wife Sarah bore a son, Isaac. While Isaac was still a boy, God put Abraham's faith and obedience to a supreme test. He told him to take his son and to sacrifice him at a shrine on the mount of Moriah. Abraham had reached the point of binding Isaac, laying him upon the altar, and taking a knife to slay him, when God called to him from heaven and told him to substitute a ram for his son. Abraham joyfully did so, and called the place "The Lord will provide."

After this Abraham sent one of his servants back to Haran to find a wife for Isaac from his wider family. At a wellside in Haran the servant met Rebecca, daughter of a nephew of Abraham. He was struck by her grace and beauty and by the hospitality her family offered him, and asked if she might be given to Isaac in marriage. She and her male relations consented, and after her journey south the marriage took place. Rebecca was childless at first, but after Abraham's death she bore twin boys, Esau first, then Jacob.

Genesis 11.27–25.26

3 JACOB AND HIS FAMILY

When Isaac was at the point of death he asked Esau to go hunting for him, so that he could enjoy a meat meal before blessing him as his elder son. Rebecca, however, disguised Jacob as Esau, and tricked her husband into blessing him instead. Once given, the blessing could not be withdrawn, and Esau was furious with his brother for denying him his birthright. So, on his parents' advice, Jacob fled to Haran. On the way north he had a dream in which he saw a ladder reaching up from earth to heaven, with angels ascending and descending upon it. God revealed himself to him, and renewed the promises he had made to Abraham.

In Haran Jacob met and fell in love with Rachel, daughter of Laban, his uncle. Jacob worked for Laban for seven years, on the basis of a promise that he could marry Rachel afterwards, but by trickery Laban contrived that he first married Rachel's elder sister, Leah. Jacob had to work for another seven years before he could marry Rachel. Then he in turn tricked Laban out of many of his animals and left, a wealthy man, to return to his own country. On his arrival he lavished gifts on Esau, and the two brothers were reconciled.

One day God appeared to Jacob, and gave him the new name of Israel. He told him that he would be father to a nation that would inhabit the lands promised to Abraham and Isaac. Israel had twelve sons by his wives and concubines; they were the ancestors of the twelve tribes of his people. Their names were Reuben, Simeon, Levi, Judah, Issachar, Zebulun, Dan, Naphtali, Gad, Asher, Joseph, and Benjamin. Israel's favorites were Joseph and Benjamin, the sons of Rachel. Rachel died giving birth to Benjamin, the youngest.

Israel's favoritism toward Joseph angered his ten older brothers, who contrived that he should be sold as a slave into Egypt and that his father should think him dead. Joseph had a checkered career in Egypt until God enabled him to interpret Pharaoh's dreams, and secured him royal favor; he became the second person in the land, and successfully steered Egypt through a prolonged period of famine that afflicted the whole region. During this famine his brothers came to Egypt to buy food. Joseph played various tricks on them before revealing who he was. Then he obtained Pharaoh's permission for the whole family to move to Egypt, where they prospered and multiplied.

Genesis 27–50

4   MOSES

After the death of Joseph the Egyptians began to worry about the growing numbers of Israelites. In consequence a new Pharaoh enslaved them, and then gave instructions that all their baby boys were to be killed. To escape this edict, an Israelite mother hid her son in a reed basket by the river Nile. He was found and rescued by Pharaoh's daughter. She brought him up as her adopted son, giving him the name Moses.

One day when Moses had grown up he came across an Egyptian who was harming one of his own people; he killed him, and in consequence had to flee to the land of Midian. There God appeared to him in a burning bush, and told him that it was his mission to lead his people out of Egypt, and back to the land promised to Abraham and his descendants. At first Moses was reluctant, but eventually he and his brother Aaron went to Pharaoh to ask him to let the Israelites go. Pharaoh's first reaction was to treat the people even more harshly, so God sent a series of plagues on Egypt, culminating in one in which the firstborn child in every family died. At God's command, however, the Israelites marked the doorposts of their houses with blood, and the angel of death passed over them. This deliverance was the origin of the Jewish feast of Passover.

Eventually Pharaoh gave the Israelites permission to depart, but barely had they gone when he changed his mind, and sent his army in pursuit of them. Guided by a pillar of cloud by day and a pillar of fire by night, the fugitives reached the Red Sea. At God's command Moses raised his staff and held his hand out over the sea. It parted, and the people passed through safely, but when Pharaoh's army sought to follow, the sea returned and drowned them.

Moses led the Israelites into the desert lands between Egypt and the promised land. The people were often hungry and thirsty, and complained bitterly; God fed them with a substance they called manna, and on one occasion Moses provided water by striking a rock with his staff. After defeating the Amalekites, a wandering tribe who stood in their way, they came to Mount Sinai, and camped there.

Exodus 1–19.2

5   THE GIVING OF THE LAW

While the Israelites were camped at Mount Sinai God came down in fire and thunder and gave Moses the Law by which they were to live. Its moral and spiritual demands were summed up in the Ten Commandments. The people were to have no other god; they were not to make or worship images; they were not to misuse the name of God; they should keep the Sabbath day (Saturday) holy; they were to honor their parents; they were forbidden to commit murder or adultery, to steal, to give false evidence, or to covet other people's possessions. Other more detailed laws governed diet, dress, personal relations, worship, and every aspect of daily life.

God made a covenant with the people of Israel: He would care for them, and they would obey his commandments. This covenant was sealed with the blood from an animal sacrifice, poured out on an altar, and scattered over the people. Then the leaders of the people accompanied Moses partway up the mountain and feasted before God; Moses alone ascended to the summit, and remained there for forty days.

While Moses was communing with God the people grew restless. They asked Aaron to make them gods of their own, and in response he took their golden ornaments and melted them into the form of a calf. God told Moses of this disobedience, and Moses pleaded successfully with him that he should not vent his fury on the people. However, when Moses came down from the mountain carrying God's commandments on two stone tablets and saw the people dancing before the calf, he was enraged. He shattered the tablets, ground the calf into dust, and used men of the tribe of Levi to kill many of those who had been disobedient.

Moses ascended the mountain again with two new tablets of stone. There he had a further vision of God, and received further commands. When he came down his face shone so brightly that thereafter he wore a veil when speaking to his people.

Under instruction from Moses the people created the Tabernacle, which was their place of worship. Within the Tabernacle lay the Holy of Holies, a sacred space that contained the Ark of the Covenant, a wooden chest. When the Tabernacle was complete the glory of the Lord descended upon it in the form of a cloud by day and fire by night. It was only when the cloud lifted that the Israelites continued their journeying.

Exodus 19–40

6   JOSHUA AND THE JUDGES

Moses led the Israelites for forty years. Eventually they came to the east bank of the river Jordan, where Moses died and Joshua succeeded him. God held back the waters of the river so that the Israelites could cross it and lay siege to the city of Jericho. For six days their army marched around the city. On the seventh they marched around it seven times; and, as the trumpets blew and the soldiers shouted, the walls of the city collapsed. The Israelites advanced into it and put the inhabitants to the sword.

In subsequent years Joshua conquered much of the promised land. Killing or enslaving many of the existing inhabitants, he settled eleven of the twelve tribes on their own land. The Levites, the priestly tribe, lived in the towns.

After Joshua's death there was no single leader of the Israelites for many years. Individual tribes conducted campaigns to enlarge their territories, and were often seduced into worship of the gods of the peoples among whom they lived. God punished them through defeat in battle; when they repented, he raised up "Judges" (military and political leaders) who delivered them from their enemies. This cycle of events repeated itself over a long period.

One notable Judge was named Gideon. He raised an army against an invasion by hostile tribes, but then dismissed most of his followers. He equipped the three hundred who remained with clay jars, torches, and trumpets, and attacked the enemy camp by night. His soldiers surrounded the camp, smashed the jars that held the lighted torches, blew their trumpets, and shouted: "A sword for the Lord and for Gideon." Panic-stricken, the enemy began fighting among themselves, and were slaughtered as they fled.

Samson, another Judge, who was under a vow and forbidden to cut his hair, was a man of immense strength who once killed a lion with his bare hands. He was in constant conflict with the Philistines, who lived to the west of the Israelites. Eventually he was captured through the treachery of Delilah, a woman with whom he was infatuated; she cut off his hair and his strength left him. The Philistines blinded and enslaved Samson, but, as his hair grew again, his strength returned. At a festival Samson was brought to the temple of the god Dagon so that the Philistines could mock him. He put his arms around the central pillars of the temple and dislodged them. The building collapsed; Samson was killed, and a multitude of Philistines with him.

Deuteronomy 34; Joshua; Judges

THE TERRITORIES OF THE TWELVE TRIBES

12 TRIBES OF ISRAEL

NEIGHBORING TRIBES

Historic Names

(Modern Names)

40 Miles

40 Kms

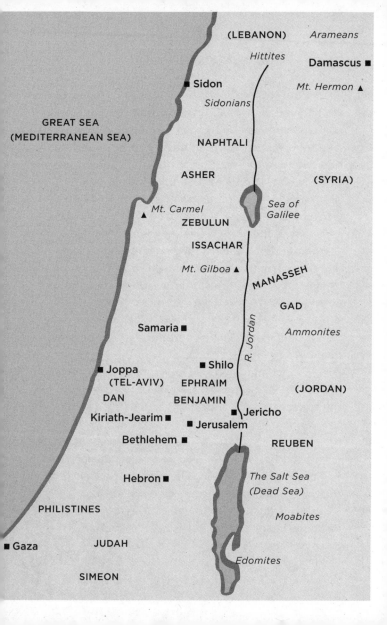

7   SAMUEL, SAUL, AND DAVID

During the time of the Judges a childless woman called Hannah went to pray at a shrine named Shiloh, served by the priest Eli. She promised that, if she were granted a child, she would dedicate him to God. Soon afterwards she bore a son whom she named Samuel; when he was of an age to leave home, she gave him to serve God in the shrine. One night God called him. At first Samuel thought Eli was summoning him, but Eli realized what was happening, and instructed him that when the call came again he was to say: "Speak, Lord, your servant is listening." He spoke as commanded, and was given the message that Eli's sons were unworthy of the priestly office.

In manhood Samuel became Judge over all Israel. He called his people back to the worship of God, and led them to victory in battle over the Philistines. However, his sons, like Eli's, proved unworthy to succeed him, and agitation grew for a king. Samuel warned the people that a king would exploit them for his own purposes and would weaken their reliance on God, but they persisted in their demand. So Samuel selected a young man named Saul from the tribe of Benjamin, and anointed him as king.

Saul quickly proved himself as a military leader, as did his son Jonathan, but they had a hard task maintaining themselves against the Philistines, and Saul angered Samuel by disobeying God's commands. Samuel therefore looked for another king, and secretly anointed David, the youngest son of Jesse of Bethlehem, from the tribe of Judah.

Saul was frequently attacked by an evil spirit. So, because David was a skilled musician, he was summoned to the court to play to Saul and to rescue him from rage and melancholy. David achieved a wider fame when he overcame the giant Goliath, a Philistine champion, killing him with a stone from a slingshot. He became a successful military leader and a close friend of Jonathan; he was given a daughter of Saul in marriage.

Saul, however, grew jealous of David, and plotted to kill him, but with Jonathan's help David escaped. He became an outlaw, constantly on the run, and eventually took service with the Philistines. He was not, though, with them at the battle of Gilboa, at which the Israelites were defeated and both Saul and Jonathan were killed. These deaths cleared the way for David to claim the throne.

1 Samuel

8   DAVID AS KING

David claimed Saul's crown with the support of the southern tribes of Judah and Benjamin, but it was only when he had defeated Saul's heirs that he was acknowledged as king by the northern tribes. After some years he captured the city of Jerusalem and made it his capital. He knew by now that God had confirmed him as king and had made him powerful so that he could govern the whole Israelite community. To make Jerusalem the center of religious worship, and to ensure the loyalty of the northern tribes, he brought the Ark to Jerusalem from its previous resting place at Kiriath-Jearim. God told him through Nathan the prophet that he was to leave building a temple to house the Ark to his successor.

In a series of wars David defeated surrounding peoples and expanded the boundaries of his kingdom from Egypt to the Euphrates. He proved himself as a statesman and administrator as well as a military leader, and was famous for his skill as a poet and musician. However, despite his deep religious faith, he disgraced himself by falling in love with Bathsheba, a married woman, and by contriving to have her husband, Uriah, killed in battle. He was severely rebuked by Nathan for marrying Bathsheba, and the first son of their marriage died. Their second son was Solomon.

David had a number of sons by other marriages. His immediate heir, Amnon, was killed by his own half-brother, Absalom, because he had raped Absalom's sister. After a period of disgrace Absalom was allowed back into the King's favor. This did not, however, prevent him from plotting a rebellion that was supported by the northern tribes, and which was initially successful. David was forced to flee from Jerusalem, but Absalom mishandled his opportunities, and was defeated in a battle fought soon afterwards. Against David's instructions, and much to his distress, Joab, the commander of his army, killed Absalom.

In the last period of his forty-year reign David consolidated his hold on his kingdom. In extreme old age he grew feeble, and his eldest surviving son Adonijah conspired with Joab, intending to claim the succession. However, Bathsheba had secured a promise from David that Solomon should become king; and, with the support of Nathan and other powerful dignitaries, she persuaded him to proclaim Solomon publicly. After succeeding to the throne, Solomon had all the chief conspirators against him put to death.

2 Samuel; 1 Kings 1–2

9   THE PSALMS

Psalms were the hymns of the Jewish people. Because David was noted as a composer, his name was attached to many of them, but they actually came from a number of pens over a long period. They were primarily intended for use in public worship, and especially for the great festivals at Jerusalem. They were sometimes sung to a secular tune and often to an instrumental accompaniment, by the people as a whole or by a choir of Levites (the servants of the Temple) with the people responding "Hallelujah" ("Praise God") or "Amen" ("So be it"). Psalm 150 paints a vivid picture of Israel at worship:

Praise God in his holy place; praise Him in the firmament of heaven.

Praise Him for his mighty deeds; praise Him in his surpassing greatness.

Praise Him in the sound of the trumpet; praise Him on harp and lyre.

Praise Him with tambourines and dancing; praise Him with strings and pipe.

Praise Him with clanging cymbals; Praise Him with loud cymbals.

Let everything that has breath; praise the Lord.

Psalms were of various kinds: hymns of praise, laments, thanksgivings, or meditations.

Several were intended for royal occasions, such as a coronation or a wedding. Some were sung at the daily Temple burnt offering, some by pilgrims on their way to and from Jerusalem, some at the Passover festival. Some expressed rage and hatred. Between them they represented the whole range of Jewish spirituality.

Psalm 23 is an expression of communion with God:

The Lord is my shepherd; I shall not want.

He makes me lie down in green pastures; he leads me beside still waters.

He restores my spirit; he leads me in the paths of righteousness for his name's sake.

Even though I walk through the valley of the shadow of death, I will fear no evil, for you are with me; your rod and staff comfort me.

You prepare a table before me in the presence of my enemies; you anoint my head with oil; my cup runs over.

Surely goodness and mercy shall follow me all the days of my life, and I shall dwell in the house of the Lord forever.

Psalms

10 SOLOMON AND THE DIVISION OF HIS KINGDOM

Early in his reign King Solomon had a dream in which God appeared to him and offered him anything he wanted. Because Solomon chose wisdom God was pleased with him, and promised him wealth and glory as well. Solomon did indeed become famous for his wisdom: for the proverbs and songs he composed, and for his knowledge of the natural world. He was a wise administrator of justice too. On one occasion two women came before him, each claiming that a baby boy was her own. Solomon called for a sword and offered to cut the boy in two, giving half to each claimant. One of the women agreed; the other said she would prefer her rival to have the living child. She, the king decided, was the real mother.

Solomon built himself a splendid palace in Jerusalem. He also built and lavishly furnished a Temple, which held the Ark and which became the center of the worship and sacrificial practice of the Israelite religion. When the Queen of Sheba in Arabia came to visit Solomon she was dazzled by the spectacle of his court.

However, splendor came at a price. To support the vast expense of his rule Solomon imposed forced labor and heavy taxation on his people, and bartered away some of the territory that David had acquired. Nor was he wholly faithful to the Israelite religion. Influenced by his many foreign wives and concubines, he built shrines for, and even worshipped, gods other than the God of Israel.

Solomon had to deal with opposition from both outside and within his kingdom. In the later years of his reign he was harassed by the rulers of neighboring countries, and he had to quell an attempt at rebellion by Jeroboam, one of his courtiers.

When Solomon died his son Rehoboam succeeded him, but Jeroboam returned from exile to confront him. The northern tribes had been harshly treated under Solomon and they sought a promise that their burdens would be lessened. Rehoboam replied, however: "My little finger is thicker than my father's loins. My father whipped you but I shall flay you." At once the northern tribes rebelled, choosing Jeroboam as their king. Rehoboam was left only with the southern territory of Judah. There was constant war between the two kingdoms, and in both, pagan gods were widely worshipped.

1 Kings 3–14

11 ELIJAH AND ELISHA

From the reign of Jeroboam onward the northern kingdom of Israel had a checkered and bloodthirsty history. Disputes over succession often resulted in the wholesale massacre of the families of the defeated contenders.

King Ahab, whose father Omri had fought his way to the throne, succeeded to it in about the year 869 B.C. Elijah the prophet condemned him because, influenced by his wife Jezebel, he worshipped the Canaanite god Baal. Elijah prophesied that God would punish Ahab with a drought. When it occurred, Elijah took refuge by a stream and was fed by ravens. When the stream dried up he was cared for by a widow. He repaid her hospitality by miraculously replenishing her scanty stock of flour and oil, and by bringing her son back to life after he had died.

Then Elijah challenged the prophets of Baal to meet him on Mount Carmel, to see who could bring an end to the drought. The prophets of Baal tried to bring rain by dancing, self-mutilation, and sacrifice, but failed. Then Elijah successfully called on God to send down fire from heaven to consume a sacrifice, and prayed for rain. It came at once, but, since Elijah had incited the people to kill the prophets of Baal, he had to flee. He came to Mount Horeb and there had a direct experience of God: not in the wind, earthquake, and fire that came down on the mountain, but as an almost inaudible voice, a sound of gentle stillness. God told him to name Elisha as his successor.

Some time later Ahab tried to acquire the vineyard of a man called Naboth. Naboth refused to sell, so, on the advice of Jezebel, Ahab arranged for him to be falsely accused and stoned to death. Ahab confiscated the vineyard, and was strongly condemned by Elijah for his wickedness.

Eventually Ahab was killed in battle, and was succeeded in turn by his sons Ahaziah and Jehoram. During the reign of Ahaziah Elijah was taken up to heaven in a chariot of fire. Elisha proved himself a worthy successor by performing miracles. Most spectacularly, he cured Naaman, commander of the king of Aram's army, of leprosy. Elisha refused to speak to Naaman in person, but sent a message that he was to wash himself seven times in the river Jordan. Naaman was indignant at this dismissive treatment, but eventually agreed to do as he had been told. His leprosy left him.

1 Kings 15–2 Kings 5

12 THE NORTHERN KINGDOM'S DOWNFALL; ISAIAH

Elisha took vengeance on the family of Ahab by arranging for Jehu, one of Jehoram's generals, to be anointed king. After being anointed, Jehu drove furiously to the town of Jezreel and murdered Jehoram. Jezebel was thrown from an upper window and her corpse eaten by dogs. All descendants of Ahab and the leading worshippers of Baal were murdered. Baal worship was stamped out, but other forms of idolatry continued.

Jehu and his descendants reigned over the northern kingdom for many years, but eventually his dynasty too was overthrown. The kingdom had an unsettled history, sometimes prospering and sometimes being defeated by neighboring peoples. At a time of relative prosperity the prophet Amos fiercely criticized the exploitation of the poor by the rich, and the prophet Hosea attacked Israel's unfaithfulness to her loving God. Both prophets taught that God valued compassion and social justice above religious rituals.

In the eighth century B.C., Assyria became the predominant power in the region. For a time the northern Kingdom survived by pursuing pro-Assyrian policies, but eventually an attempt to throw off the Assyrian yoke resulted in the siege of the capital, Samaria, and its capture in the year 721 B.C. Many citizens were deported, and the northern kingdom ceased to exist.

Meanwhile the southern kingdom of Judah had a less turbulent history. For the most part it was ruled by descendants of David; often they worked closely with the priests of the Temple, and tried, though without total success, to do away with pagan worship. Like the northern kingdom, Judah was forced to pay tribute to Assyria; a defiant alliance with Egypt provoked an invasion and a siege of Jerusalem, which the monarchy was fortunate to survive. The prophet Isaiah, who lived at this time, attacked the vices of the rich and powerful, and advocated a policy of neutrality rather than one of entering into alliances hostile to Assyria. He prophesied the coming of the Messiah, a descendant of David who would rule in justice and mercy over a restored Israel.

King Josiah, who reigned in the first part of the seventh century B.C., reformed religious practice. The contents of a scroll discovered in the Temple in Jerusalem provided the basis for a return to purity of worship and behavior. Religious sites dedicated to other gods were destroyed and the importance of the Temple enhanced. However, Josiah was defeated and killed when he tried to prevent an Egyptian invasion, and his reforms proved to be short-lived.

2 Kings 8–23.30; Amos; Hosea; Isaiah 1–39

13 JONAH

The story of Jonah is set at a time when the empire of Assyria was at its height. God commanded the prophet Jonah to go to the Assyrian capital of Nineveh, to condemn its people for their wickedness. To escape this command, and to put himself (as he hoped) out of God's reach, Jonah boarded a ship going from Joppa to Tarshish. But during the journey God sent a great storm. The sailors prayed to their gods and threw things overboard to lighten the ship. Still fearing for their safety, they cast lots to discover who was to blame for their misfortune. The lot fell on Jonah, who confessed that he had been trying to escape the true God who had made heaven and earth. He suggested that the crew throw him overboard, and, having tried in vain to reach the land, they did so; at once the storm subsided. Jonah was swallowed by a great fish, and spent three days inside it before being cast up on the shore.

Realizing the folly of disobedience, Jonah obeyed a second command from God: He went to Nineveh and prophesied its destruction. King and people alike accepted his message; they repented, fasted, and clothed themselves and their animals in sackcloth. Consequently God withheld his punishment of them. Jonah was very angry because his prophecy had been set aside, and reproached God for his compassion and generosity. He went outside the city, took shelter in the shade of a bush that God provided, and sulked.

The next day God struck the bush and it withered. Jonah was exposed to the full heat of the sun and to a scorching wind; he was so overcome that he prayed for death. God asked him if he was angry that the bush had withered. Jonah replied that he was furious, to which God responded: "If you are so upset about a bush which came up one day and died the next, am I not entitled to be sorry for the 120,000 people of Nineveh in their ignorance and helplessness?"

Jonah

14 THE SOUTHERN KINGDOM'S DOWNFALL; JEREMIAH

King Josiah's defeat at the hands of Pharaoh Necho resulted in the imposition of a puppet monarchy in the southern Kingdom of Judah, and in the payment of tribute. Egypt was however unable to protect Judah from the increasingly powerful empire of Babylon, which replaced Assyria as the dominant power in the region. Judah became a satellite state to Babylon; then, after a revolt, the Babylonians besieged Jerusalem, captured it in 597 B.C., and took away King Jehoiachin and large numbers of leading citizens to captivity in Babylon. A few years later the puppet King Zedekiah, whom the Babylonians had installed, also revolted. After a second siege, Jerusalem was taken again, its walls and the Temple destroyed, and more of the population deported. A third revolt, in which the Babylonian governor of Judah was murdered, also failed, and its leaders fled into Egypt.

When they fled they took with them the prophet Jeremiah, the greatest religious figure of his age. He came from a priestly family, but in his teaching he had fiercely attacked the presumption that the Temple in Jerusalem guaranteed the city's safety. He had also attacked the king and his entourage for the social injustices that they permitted and perpetrated. With regard to foreign policy, he had advocated neutrality between Egypt and Babylon and, later, submission to Babylon as the least damaging courses of action to follow. In a letter to the exiles in Babylon he had urged them to seek peace for themselves and for the city in which they now lived.

Jeremiah had a deep sense of God, and a personal but agonizing relationship with him. Much of his teaching was concerned with sin and judgment, and only occasionally did he look forward to happier times to come. He was deeply unpopular with his own people, and suffered greatly at their hands. His advice was scoffed at and ignored; some of his prophecies, which had been written down by the scribe Baruch, were burned by the king in person; he was beaten and placed in the stocks; during the siege of Jerusalem he was imprisoned and for a time cast into a muddy pit. His enforced exile in Egypt was the final episode in a life full of tragedy but also of inspired teaching and dogged faithfulness.

2 Kings 23.29–26; Jeremiah

The people from the southern Kingdom who had been deported to Babylon were not badly treated, and some of them prospered. However, they had to rethink their beliefs in the light of the disaster that had befallen them, and were helped to do so by two prophets.

The first was Ezekiel, a priest who prophesied both to the Jews in exile and to those remaining in the Holy Land. He condemned his people for their disloyalty to their covenant with God, and saw himself as a watchman warning against impending disaster. He stressed individual as well as communal responsibility. He preached judgment, but also looked forward to the restoration of Israel. In a vision he saw a valley of dry bones; the bones first became bodies and then had life breathed into them. The meaning of the vision was that through God's Spirit the Jewish people would be brought to life again, and restored to their own land.

The second prophet, whose teaching is recorded in the later chapters of the book of Isaiah, wrote from Babylon during the time when it began to decline. His message was one of hope and encouragement. He looked forward to the empire's overthrow by the Persians and to the return of the exiles to their own land. Several passages in his writing refer to a servant who would be led like a lamb to the slaughter, who would suffer on behalf of others, and by his suffering redeem them.

In 539 B.C. Babylon fell to the Persians, whose policy it was to send exiles back to their own lands and to encourage local customs of worship. In ensuing years groups of Jews returned to the area of the southern kingdom and began the rebuilding of the Temple in Jerusalem, a work completed in 515 B.C. The prophets Haggai and Zechariah encouraged the people in this achievement. Zechariah was one of several prophets who expected a Messiah who would reign over a purified Israel, which would be a light to the whole world.

Two great leaders, Ezra and Nehemiah, were sent by the Persian government to set the Jewish community in order. Ezra, a priest, reimposed the Jewish law; Nehemiah, a secular leader, rebuilt the walls of Jerusalem and tried to improve the lot of the poor. Both leaders tried to re-create a God-centered nation and to prevent mixed marriages; the effect of their work was to divide the Jewish community in the south from the other peoples in the promised land.

Ezekiel; Isaiah 40–55; Haggai;
Zechariah; Ezra; Nehemiah

16   THE WRITINGS:
JOB AND ECCLESIASTES

The pre-Christian books of the Bible fall into four groups—the Pentateuch (the first five books), the Former and Latter Prophets (the books dealing with history and prophecy), and the Writings. Among the Writings are Psalms and Proverbs, the Song of Solomon (a book of love poems), Job, and Ecclesiastes.

The book of Job explores the huge issue of undeserved suffering. It tells of a wealthy man blessed with a large family, who lived a virtuous and godly life. In conversation with one of his servants, Satan, God spoke well of Job. Satan, whose responsibility it was to act as the accuser of humankind, replied that Job's virtue was simply due to his prosperity. God therefore gave him permission to harass Job, though without harming him personally. So Satan deprived Job of his wealth and of his children; but Job, though grieving, accepted his fate, and said: "The Lord gives and the Lord takes away; blessed be the name of the Lord."

Then God gave Satan permission to afflict Job physically. He contracted sores from head to foot, and sat among ashes scraping himself with a shard of pottery. When three friends came to visit him, Job burst out in a terrible lament. One after another his friends tried to explain his affliction. Their main argument was that in some way he must have deserved it, but Job vehemently denied that this was so. Eventually, God revealed himself to Job in person, in all his creative splendor. Job exclaimed: "I knew of you only by report, but now I see you with my own eyes," and submitted to him. God rewarded him by restoring his wealth and giving him a new family.

The book of Ecclesiastes was written by a teacher of wisdom reflecting in a spirit of free inquiry on the problems that life presents. Its message is that life is basically futile, since in the long run nothing changes: "Vanity of vanities, all is vanity." Even reflection is empty: "In much wisdom is much vexation; the more knowledge, the more suffering." One should make the best of this life, since it is all one has. There is a right time for everything, but no way of understanding God's purposes as a whole. Nonetheless, one should "Fear God and obey his commandments."

Job; Ecclesiastes

17 THE CENTURIES BEFORE THE COMING OF JESUS

Many years after the event, stories were told of the heroism of the exiles living in Babylon during the period of captivity there. One story was about Shadrach, Meshach, and Abednego, who were thrown into a fiery furnace because of their refusal to worship an idol set up by King Nebuchadnezzar. Assisted by an angel, they survived without harm, and from then on the King protected them in their religious practices.

Another story concerned a Jewish exile called Daniel. While King Belshazzar was giving a great feast, writing mysteriously appeared on the wall of his palace. None of the King's magicians were able to interpret the writing, but Daniel correctly told him that it pronounced doom upon his kingdom because of his idolatry.

In a third story King Darius the Mede, who by then had captured Babylon, was persuaded by some of his courtiers to issue an edict that no one was to pray to anyone save himself. Daniel, now a leading royal servant, continued his practice of daily public prayer to the true God, and was condemned to be thrown into a den of lions. His faith ensured that he survived unharmed, and the enemies who had plotted his death were subjected to the fate they had intended for him.

A series of visions were granted to Daniel; between them they revealed the destiny of his people. The visions related to the rise and fall of successive empires, culminating in the conquest of Persia by Alexander the Great. After Alexander's death in 323 B.C. there was a long period of instability, during which there were attempts to stamp out traditional Jewish practices. The stories about Daniel and the visions attributed to him were an inspiration to those Jews determined to remain true to their faith.

Some versions of the Bible say nothing about the period between Alexander's conquests and the reign of Herod the Great, King of Judea, which began in 37 B.C. Others include the Apocrypha, a collection of books dealing with those years. It was a time of constant warfare. When Herod the Great came to the throne it was as a nominee of the Romans, who were by then the dominant power in the whole Mediterranean area. It was also a time during which there was increasing expectation that a Messiah would come.

Daniel

18 THE VISIONS OF ZECHARIAH AND MARY

During the reign of Herod the Great a priest called Zechariah had a vision while he was on duty in the temple in Jerusalem. An angel told him that he and his wife Elizabeth would have a son who was to be called John, meaning "The Lord is gracious." This would happen even though they were both past the normal age of childbearing. Zechariah doubted this divine message; in consequence he lost the power of speech.

Soon afterwards Elizabeth conceived. When she was six months pregnant a young relation of hers, called Mary, was visited by an angel, who told her that she had been chosen by God to give birth to a son. He would be called the Son of God, and would become a king of David's line forever. Mary exclaimed: "How can this happen? I am still a virgin." The angel replied "The conception will be the work of the Holy Spirit." Mary accepted the angel's message, and went to share her good news with Elizabeth. Elizabeth blessed Mary for her faith and told her that when she arrived she felt her own child leap within her.

Mary rejoiced with these words:

"My soul praises God and my spirit rejoices in God my Savior, because he has chosen a lowly young woman to be the instrument of his saving power.

From now on, everyone shall call me blessed; for the holy and mighty God has done great things for me.

God has shown his mercy upon succeeding generations, upon all who fear him.

In his strength he has defeated the proud and their schemes, humbling the powerful and exalting the humble, feeding the hungry and sending the rich away empty.

He has fulfilled his ancient promises to the people of Israel, and he has shown mercy to Abraham's children forever."

When Elizabeth's baby was born, after Mary had returned to her home, local people expected that he would be called Zechariah after his father. However, because of God's message to her husband, Elizabeth insisted that he should be called John. When they asked Zechariah what he thought, he took a writing tablet and supported his wife. Immediately he was able to speak again, and prophesied that his son would be the forerunner of someone even greater.

Luke 1

Mary was engaged to a carpenter called Joseph, who lived in the town of Nazareth in the northern province of Galilee, and who was a just and upright man. When he discovered she was pregnant his first intention was to separate from her. Then an angel appeared to him in a dream, told him of the child's divine origin, and commanded him to call the child "Jesus," which means "God saves." Joseph was obedient to this vision. He took Mary as his wife, but they did not consummate their marriage until her son was born.

At that time the Roman Emperor Augustus ordered a census. Because he was a descendant of King David, Joseph returned to David's native city of Bethlehem to register, taking the pregnant Mary with him. Jesus was born in Bethlehem, in a stable because the inn was full.

An angel appeared to a group of shepherds grazing their flocks nearby. They were terrified, but the angel told them that he came with good news. The Christ (that is, the anointed king) had been born in Bethlehem; they would find him wrapped in strips of cloth and lying in a manger. Then a great host of angels appeared, praising God and promising peace to those he favored. The shepherds went to Bethlehem, visited the family, and spread the news that this was a very special baby. After eight days he was circumcised and the name Jesus formally conferred upon him.

A few weeks later Jesus' parents took him to the Temple in Jerusalem to perform the rites associated with the birth of a first-born son. While they were there two holy people—a man called Simeon and an elderly woman called Anna—blessed Jesus and foresaw a great destiny for him. Simeon prayed:

"Lord, now permit your servant to die in peace, according to your promise.

For I have seen the salvation which you have prepared before all the nations, to serve as a revelation to those who are not Jews, and to glorify your own people, Israel."

Simeon warned Mary that suffering lay ahead, for her son and for herself, while Anna talked about him to everyone hoping for the deliverance of the people of Israel.

Matthew 1.18–25; Luke 2.1–38

While the holy family were still living in Bethlehem, wise men from the east came in search of a newly born king of the Jews. They were guided by a star, but they also sought help from King Herod. He was alarmed by their mission, but, after consultation with religious leaders, he directed them to Bethlehem, where the prophet Micah had foretold a king would be born. He inquired when the star guiding them had appeared, and asked them to return to him when they had found the child, so that he too could pay homage to him. The wise men followed the star to Bethlehem, visited the holy family, worshipped the child, and presented him with gifts of gold, incense, and myrrh.

Suspecting Herod's intentions, the wise men returned home another way, while Joseph was warned in a dream to take his wife and child to safety in Egypt. It was as well he did so, since Herod, in fear for his throne, ordered a massacre of all boys under the age of two in the Bethlehem region. It was not until Herod died that Joseph was able to take his family back to his own country, to live in Nazareth.

When Jesus reached the age of twelve he went with his family and friends to Jerusalem for the annual feast of Passover. On the journey home his family did not miss him until they had gone some distance. Immediately they returned to Jerusalem and spent three days searching for him. At last they found him in the Temple, engaged in discussion with the teachers there, and astonishing them with his intelligence. His mother asked: "Why have you treated us like this? Your father and I have been looking for you anxiously." Jesus replied: "Did you not realize I would be in my Father's house?" Then he went back to Nazareth with them, remained an obedient son in the family home, and followed the trade of a carpenter until he was about thirty years old.

Matthew 2; Mark 6.3; Luke 2.41–52, 3.23

21 JESUS' BAPTISM AND TEMPTATIONS

John, son of Zechariah and Elizabeth, chose to live an austere life in the Judean desert. He wore a garment of camel's hair and lived on locusts and wild honey. He preached a demanding message in which he offered baptism with water as a sign of repentance and the forgiveness of sins. Huge crowds came to hear him, and were baptized in the River Jordan. When Jewish spiritual leaders joined those coming to be baptized, John told them not to rely on their Israelite heritage for salvation, but to lead better lives. He prophesied that there was someone far greater than himself coming after him, whose sandals he was unworthy to remove. This greater one would baptize, not with water, but with the life of God, the Holy Spirit.

Jesus was among those who offered themselves for baptism. At first John tried to dissuade him, saying: "It is I who need to be baptized by you." Eventually, however, Jesus persuaded him to perform the ceremony by saying: "We should do everything which God requires." So John baptized Jesus; as he came up from the water the Holy Spirit descended upon him in the form of a dove, and a voice from heaven declared: "This is my son, the Beloved, with whom I am well pleased."

Then the Holy Spirit led Jesus into the desert, where he spent forty days fasting and praying. During that time the devil appeared to him and tried to persuade him to misuse the special powers that God had given him, but he resisted successfully, relying on the guidance of the Scriptures, the sacred writings of the Jewish faith. Tempted, in his hunger, to turn stones into bread, he replied: "Man does not live only by bread, but by the word of God." Tempted to throw himself down from the parapet of the Temple in Jerusalem, relying on angels to protect him, he replied: "Scripture says you should not put God to the test." Tempted to become an earthly king at the price of doing the devil homage, he replied: "You shall worship God alone." Then the devil left him, and angels came and ministered to him.

Soon after he had baptized Jesus, John was arrested and thrown into prison for criticizing Herod, ruler of the province of Galilee and son of Herod the Great, for marrying his close relation Herodias.

Matthew 3, 4; Mark 1.14, 6.17–18

After John's arrest Jesus began his active ministry. His message was: "The time has come; the rule of God is close at hand; repent and believe the good news."

For his first disciples Jesus called from their nets two pairs of fishermen—Simon (whom he nicknamed Peter—"the Rock") and Andrew, sons of Jonah, and James and John, sons of Zebedee. He soon became well known and much talked about. People from a wide area came to hear his teaching and to be healed of sickness. However, when he brought his message to his hometown of Nazareth he ran into trouble. In an address in the synagogue (the local place of worship), he quoted words of the prophet Isaiah:

"The Spirit of the Lord is upon me because he has anointed me;he has sent me to announce good news to the poor,

to proclaim release for prisoners and recovery of sight for the blind;

to proclaim the year of the Lord's favor."

He then told his hearers that this prophecy was being fulfilled that very day. Remembering his humble background, they were astonished at his implied claim that he was, at the least, a prophet. When Jesus rebuked them for their lack of faith, they reacted with such hostility that he barely escaped with his life.

From his prison John heard about the progress of Jesus' ministry. He sent two of his followers to ask Jesus: "Are you the One we are expecting, or is he still to come?" Jesus replied indirectly, by pointing to his healing work and to the good news he was bringing to the poor, and by saying: "Happy is he who has no doubts about me."

Herod stood in awe of John, and liked to listen to his teaching. His wife Herodias, however, hated John because of his opposition to her marriage. During Herod's birthday celebrations, a dance by Herodias' daughter so delighted him that he offered her anything she wanted. At her mother's instigation she asked for the head of John on a plate. Reluctantly, Herod ordered his execution. John's head was given to the girl, and she gave it to her mother.

Mark 1.14–45, 6.14–29;
Luke 3.23, 4.16–30, 7.18–23

PROVINCES AT THE TIME OF JESUS

PROVINCES

Historic Names

(Modern Names)

40 Miles

40 Kms

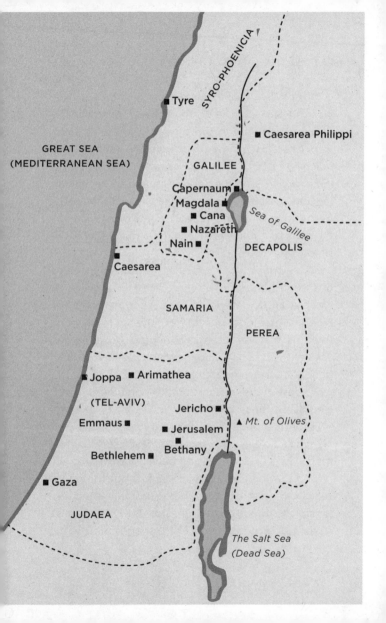

23   JESUS' MINISTRY CONTINUES

Initially Jesus ministered in his home province of Galilee, in the north of the promised land. In the synagogue in the town of Capernaum he astonished his fellow worshippers one Sabbath, by teaching on his own authority rather than by relying exclusively on the Scriptures, and by healing a man possessed by a demon. That same day he performed other miracles of healing, and many more in the days that followed. He cured a man of leprosy simply by touching him.

He tried to avoid publicity for his miracles, but nonetheless crowds gathered wherever he went. A group carrying a paralyzed man went so far as to break open a roof in order to lower him to Jesus' feet for healing. On another occasion, to escape the crush, he taught from a boat while the people stood on the shore.

Jesus soon became involved in controversy. He gave offense by forgiving sins, a power that most Jews thought was reserved to God alone. He also mixed freely with social outcasts, such as the men who collected taxes on behalf of the Romans, saying that he came to call sinners, not the righteous. On occasions when others fasted, he and his disciples did not do so. He said: "A bridegroom's friends do not fast while the bridegroom is with them. While the bridegroom is present, it is right to feast; the time for fasting will come when the bridegroom has been taken away."

Jesus gave priority to human need over the detailed demands of the Jewish Law. He said: "The Sabbath was made for man, not man for the Sabbath: the Son of Man [by whom he meant himself] is Lord even of the Sabbath." Accepting a direct challenge from his critics, he healed a man with a withered arm in a synagogue on the Sabbath day. His opponents accused him of being possessed by an evil spirit, to which he retorted: "If I am driving evil spirits out of people by means of an evil spirit, then the reign of evil is about to collapse."

Mark 1–3

24   JESUS CHOOSES THE TWELVE

After spending a night in prayer, Jesus picked out from his followers twelve men whom he named apostles, a word meaning "those who are sent." They included the two pairs of brothers already mentioned—Peter and Andrew, and James and John; Jesus nicknamed the latter "sons of thunder." Matthew, whom Jesus had also called from his work to follow him, was a tax-gatherer, a member of a despised profession. Other apostles were Philip, Bartholomew, Thomas the twin, James son of Alphaeus, Judas son of James, and Simon, who had been a member of the Jewish armed resistance. Finally there was Judas Iscariot, who was later to betray him. Jesus was also attended by a group of women, some of whom he had healed, who cared for him and for the Twelve out of their own resources. They included Mary from the town of Magdala and Joanna, wife of King Herod's steward. Other followers, in larger or smaller numbers, came and went from time to time.

Jesus made it very clear that loyalty to himself overrode all other loyalties. For example, when members of his family, fearing that he was out of his mind, came to take him home, he refused to go to them, saying: "Whoever does the will of God is my brother and sister and mother."

In due course Jesus sent the Twelve out two by two to preach and heal as he was doing. He told them to take nothing except a staff for the journey—no food, no wallet, no money, and no change of clothing. They were to rely on the hospitality of others to meet their needs.

Later still Jesus sent out seventy-two of his followers on a similar mission and with the same instructions. He told them that whoever listened to them listened to him, and whoever rejected them rejected him. The seventy-two returned rejoicing in their success. Jesus rejoiced with them, and thanked his Father in heaven who had revealed to common people what was hidden from the learnéd. He added: "Everything is entrusted to me by my Father. Only the Father knows who the Son is, and only the Son and those whom the Son instructs truly know the Father."

Matthew 9.9; Mark 3.17, 3.31-35, 6.7–13; Luke 6.12–16, 8.1–3, 10.1–24

Much of Jesus' teaching was brought together when, seated on a hillside, he spoke to his disciples about life in the kingdom of God. He taught that true happiness comes from having the right attitudes. Those who are humble, concerned about the world's sinfulness, gentle, devoted to goodness, merciful, single-minded in God's service, and peace-lovers will be blessed by God. Those of his followers who are persecuted in this world should rejoice, because they will have a rich reward in the next.

Jesus emphasized that he had not come to destroy the moral demands of the Jewish Law but to fulfill them. He taught that it is not enough not to commit murder; the anger that can lead to murder must be set aside too. It is not enough not to commit adultery; lustful thoughts must be set aside too. It is not enough to keep only our solemn promises; we should always mean what we say.

The Jewish Law taught that retaliation should be proportionate to the harm done—an eye for an eye and a tooth for a tooth—but Jesus taught that we should love our enemies and that we should return good for evil, turning the other cheek when others attack us.

He went on to say that ostentatious piety and charitable giving are wrong; both piety and giving should be between ourselves and God. No one can serve two masters; it is impossible to serve both God and money. God knows what people's needs are and will supply them, in the same way as he provides food for birds and glorious clothing for flowers; we should not be anxious but should trust him. We should not judge others, for we shall be judged to the degree we judge. It is difficult to find the way to the kingdom of heaven and there will be those who will try to mislead us. We should assess others by the moral and spiritual quality of their lives.

He summarized the whole moral teaching of the Old Testament in the command to treat others as you would like them to treat you.

Jesus said that anyone who acts on his words is like a wise man who built his house on a rock. When storms came, the house stood firm. But anyone who does not act on his words is like a man who built his house on sand. When storms came, the house fell, and the ensuing devastation was great.

Matthew 5–7

26   TEACHING ON PRAYER

Both in the Sermon on the Mount and at other times Jesus taught about prayer. Personal prayer is a private matter and should not be paraded in front of others. Prayer offered in faith always receives an answer. "Ask, and you will receive; seek, and you will find; knock, and the door will be opened to you." There is no point in aimless repetition, since God knows what you need before you tell him, but perseverance in prayer is a virtue. Jesus drove this point home by telling a story about a widow who so pestered an unjust judge that finally, in exasperation, he gave her her due. If a man of that kind would behave in that way, is it likely that God will ignore those who cry out to him day and night?

Jesus taught his followers to pray in these words:

"Our Father in heaven, hallowed be your name.
Your kingdom come and your will be done,
on earth as it is in heaven.
Give us this day our daily bread,
and forgive us the wrong we have done,
just as we have forgiven those who have wronged us.
And do not bring us to the time of testing,
but rescue us from the evil one."

Jesus taught that effective prayer depends upon humility. He told a story about a Pharisee and a tax-gatherer praying in the Temple. The Pharisee prayed: "I thank you, God, that I am not greedy, dishonest, or adulterous as other people are, or like this tax-gatherer. I fast regularly and pay my religious taxes." The tax-gatherer did not even dare look up, but beat his breast saying: "God, have mercy on me, a sinner." Of the two, it was the tax-gatherer who went home forgiven.

Jesus set a personal example of prayer. He frequently went away into seclusion for extended times of prayer. His cures were often accompanied by prayer, and he passed the evening of his final arrest largely in prayer. First, in the upper room, he prayed for his friends and followers; then, in the Garden of Gethsemane, he prayed for himself.

Matthew 6.5–13, 14.23;
Luke 11.9, 18.1–14, 22.39–46;
John 17

27 PARABLES

Much of Jesus' teaching was in parables—memorable stories, drawn from people's everyday experience, which convey a spiritual meaning.

He spoke, for example, of a sower scattering seed widely over a field. Some fell on the footpath and was quickly eaten by birds. Some fell on rocky ground with little soil; it sprang up quickly but soon withered under the sun's rays. Some fell among thistles that choked it as it grew, and some fell on good ground and produced an abundant crop.

Jesus later explained to his disciples that the seed was the word of God. Some hear it and immediately forget it. Some receive it with enthusiasm, but have no staying power. Some receive it, but it is soon choked by worldly cares and pleasures; and some accept it and bear the fruit of lives pleasing to God.

To a lawyer who asked him who should count as a neighbor, he responded with a parable about a man who was attacked on a lonely road by robbers who left him half-dead. When they saw the victim, both a priest and a Temple servant passed by on the other side of the road and did nothing to help him. But a Samaritan (a man from a community the Jews hated and despised) took pity on him. He tended his wounds, took him to an inn, and paid the innkeeper to take care of him. "Which of the three," asked Jesus, "was neighbor to the man who had been attacked?" The lawyer replied: "The one who showed him kindness." Jesus concluded: "Go and do as he did."

To illustrate the generous love of God, Jesus told a story about a landowner who had two sons. One day the younger son asked for his inheritance and then went away and wasted it on foolish and extravagant living. Having lost everything, he decided to return home and to throw himself on his father's mercy. When he was still a long way away his father saw him coming, ran to meet him, forgave him on the spot, and arranged a huge party for him. This infuriated the elder son, who had stayed at home and worked hard, never stepping out of line. He complained bitterly to his father about the fact that his brother was being treated more generously than himself. In reply his father reminded him that he was heir to the whole estate, but insisted that it was right to rejoice when a lost child came home.

Mark 4.1–20; Luke 10.25–37, 15.11–32

During his ministry Jesus was often questioned: by his disciples, by those genuinely anxious to learn from him, and by those trying to trap him. Asked by some strict Jews why his disciples did not observe the laws relating to ritual cleanliness, such as the symbolic washing of hands before a meal, he replied that it was easy to concentrate on such matters and to ignore the demands of the moral law. As regards dietary restrictions, he taught that it was not what people took in that harmed them but what came out of them—the evil thoughts, words, and deeds that come from the human heart.

Jesus was also asked about divorce. He replied that the permission to divorce given in the law of Moses had been a concession to human weakness. God's will is that a man and his wife should no longer be two persons but one. Human beings should not divide those whom God has joined. Anyone who divorces and remarries commits adultery.

To a rich man who asked what he should do to obtain eternal life, Jesus replied that he should keep the moral commandments given through Moses. Assured by the man that he already did so, Jesus advised him to sell everything he had, to give the proceeds to the poor, and to follow him.

The man went away sadly. Jesus reflected that it was easier for a camel to pass through the eye of a needle than for a wealthy person to enter the kingdom of God. However, those who leave everything to follow him will be richly rewarded, in this world and the next.

His disciples asked him: "Who is greatest in the kingdom of heaven?" Jesus set a child in front of them, and said: "Unless you become as humble as a child you will never enter the kingdom of heaven. Those who are like children will be greatest in the kingdom of heaven, and whoever receives a child in my name receives me."

Peter asked Jesus: "How many times should I forgive someone who has sinned against me? Seven times?" "No," said Jesus: "seventy times seven." To expand the point he told a story about a king who forgave one of his servants a fortune, only to discover that the servant immediately demanded the repayment of a much smaller debt from a fellow servant. The king punished the unforgiving servant; similarly, God will punish us for our offenses against him unless we forgive others for their offenses against us.

Mark 7.1–23, 10.1–31;
Matthew 18.1–5, 21–35

During his travels Jesus was sometimes asked to perform miracles in order to demonstrate his powers, but he always refused, performing miracles only in response to real need. He tried to avoid them becoming general knowledge, but they often did so, filling those who saw or heard about them with amazement and awe.

On one occasion he was confronted by a man possessed by demons, who had proved uncontrollable and who lived in a graveyard. As was often the case, the demons recognized Jesus for whom he was, calling him "Son of the Most High God." When Jesus cast them out of the man they took refuge in a nearby herd of pigs, which stampeded into the sea.

As in the instance just given, Jesus sometimes cured simply with a word of command. Sometimes, however, he employed physical methods. Asked to heal a man who was deaf and who had an impediment in his speech, he put his fingers in the man's ears and touched his tongue with spittle. In the course of healing a blind man he spat on his eyes and laid his hands on him. When the man's sight returned only partially, he again laid hands on him to complete the cure.

Jesus possessed a power that other people's faith could draw upon. One day, as he was moving among a dense crowd, a woman who had suffered from bleeding for twelve years, and whom doctors had been quite unable to help, broke Jewish laws that forbade her to come close to other people and touched his cloak. Immediately she was cured. Jesus realized that power had left him, and asked who had touched him. Full of fear, the woman came forward and confessed what she had done. Jesus responded: "My daughter, your faith has healed you. Go in peace."

In Jerusalem, as in Galilee, Jesus fell foul of the religious authorities because he healed on the Sabbath. Coming across a man who had been paralyzed for thirty-eight years, and who had tried unsuccessfully to take advantage of the curative properties of the pool of Bethesda, he commanded him to take up his mattress and walk. The man did so, but, because the healing had been on the Sabbath day, Jesus was challenged about it. His explanation—"My Father continues to work, and I must work too"—gave further offense, because he was seen as making himself equal to God.

Matthew 16.1–4; Mark 5.1–20, 8.22–6, 5.25–34; John 5.1–18

30 RAISING THE DEAD

On three recorded occasions during his ministry Jesus brought dead, or apparently dead, people back to life.

Approaching the town of Nain in Galilee he came across the funeral procession of a young man, the only son of a widowed mother. Filled with compassion for her, Jesus laid his hand on the bier, and halted the procession. Then he said: "Young man, get up." To the astonishment of the crowd, the man sat up and began to speak; Jesus restored him to his mother.

On another occasion he was approached by the president of a local synagogue, a man called Jairus. He asked him to come and lay hands on his twelve-year-old daughter, who was at death's door. Jesus consented, but on the way messengers came to tell him that the girl had died. Nonetheless Jesus continued to the house, and rebuked the mourners, telling them that the girl was only asleep. They laughed at him, but he went into the room where the girl lay, took her hand, and told her to get up. She rose at once, and Jesus told her parents to give her a meal.

Some close friends of Jesus—Lazarus and his sisters, Martha and Mary—lived in the village of Bethany near Jerusalem. One day he received an urgent message from the two women to say that Lazarus was very ill, but he did not set out toward Bethany until two days later. By the time he and his disciples reached the village, Lazarus had been buried for four days. First Martha and then Mary met Jesus, and claimed that, had he been there, Lazarus would not have died. Jesus responded to Martha by saying: "I am the resurrection and the life; anyone believing in me will live, even after dying." Then, deeply moved by the sisters' distress, he asked to be taken to the tomb. He ordered the removal of the stone covering its entrance, prayed briefly, and cried: "Lazarus, come out." The dead man emerged still wrapped in his grave clothes. Jesus commanded: "Free him, and let him go."

This miracle caused a major sensation. When they heard of it, the Jewish leadership feared that Jesus would soon attract mass support and impel the Roman occupiers into a violent reaction. The high priest Caiaphas said: "It is in our interest that one man should die, rather than that the nation should be destroyed"; and from then on the leadership plotted his death.

Luke 7.11–17; Mark 5.21–24, 35–43;
John 11.1–53

31   NATURE MIRACLES

Jesus' miracles were not confined to delivering people from sickness and death. Early in his ministry he, his mother, and his disciples were guests at a wedding in Cana in Galilee when the supply of wine ran low. Jesus told the house servants to fill some large jars, usually used for ritual washing, with water. When the water was poured out it had turned to wine. The president of the feast commented that the wine was of a better quality than that which had previously been served.

One day when Simon (called Peter) and his friends had spent a fruitless night fishing, Jesus told them to try again. This time they hauled in such a catch that their nets broke and their boats began to sink. Amazed, Peter fell at Jesus' feet, and exclaimed: "Leave me, Lord, for I am a sinner." Jesus replied: "Do not be afraid; from now on you will be catching people."

After Jesus had spent a day teaching, he and his disciples were crossing the Sea of Galilee when a storm arose. Jesus was asleep in the stern of the boat, but, in fear of death, his disciples aroused him. He rebuked them for their lack of faith, and calmed the wind and the waves with the words: "Peace! be still!" In awe the disciples commented: "Who can this man be? Even the wind and the sea obey him."

On one occasion a great crowd gathered to hear him in a desert place. As evening drew on, his disciples suggested the people should go away and buy food. Jesus said: "You give them something to eat." The disciples replied that they had no more than five loaves and two fishes. Nevertheless Jesus commanded the crowd to sit down in groups, blessed the food, and divided it. Not only was there sufficient for the five thousand who were there, but twelve baskets of fragments were collected afterwards.

After this miracle he sent his disciples ahead of him by boat across Lake Galilee, while he remained behind to pray. As the boat struggled against the wind in the darkness of the night, the disciples saw Jesus walking past them on the water. Thinking it was a ghost, they were terrified and cried out. He reassured them, and, as he joined them in the boat, the wind died away.

John 2.1–12; Luke 5.1–11;
Mark 4.35–41, 6.30–52

From the earliest days of his ministry there was speculation about how Jesus fitted into Jewish religious expectations.

When he and his disciples were in the territory to the north of the Sea of Galilee, on the way to the villages of Caesarea Philippi, he asked what people were saying about him. The disciples replied that some thought that he was John the Baptist or Elijah come again, some that he was a prophet. When he asked them who they thought he was, Peter replied: "You are the Messiah." Jesus accepted the title, but ordered his disciples to say nothing about it in public. Then he began to teach them that he was a Messiah who must endure suffering and rejection, who would be put to death and then rise again. Peter found this teaching hard to accept. He remonstrated with Jesus, who rebuked him severely for thinking in human rather than in divine terms. He told the disciples that following him involved sharing his suffering: "Anyone who wants to save his life will lose it, but anyone who loses his life for my sake, and for the sake of the good news I bring, will save it."

Some days later Jesus took Peter, James, and John up a mountain. There they saw him transfigured: his clothes became dazzling white, and glory shone around him. Moses and Elijah appeared to them and spoke with Jesus. The disciples were awestruck and terrified. Then a cloud overshadowed them, and a voice from heaven declared: "This is my beloved son; listen to him"; at that the vision disappeared. Afterwards, as they descended the hillside, Jesus told the disciples to say nothing about what had happened until he had risen from the dead, a concept they found difficult to grasp. They asked him what the Scriptures meant by saying that Elijah must come first, to set everything right. Jesus replied that Elijah had already come, in the person of John the Baptist.

When they rejoined the other disciples, they found them surrounded by a crowd arguing with them over their failure to cure an epileptic boy. Jesus talked with the boy's father, who described the terrible effects of his son's illness and then cried: "Lord I believe; help my unbelief." Jesus cured the boy, and later told his disciples that some illnesses would respond only to prayer.

Mark 8.27–9.27; Matthew 11.14

33   JESUS' TRUE NATURE

It was not until Jesus had risen from the dead that his followers began fully to understand his true nature. What that nature was is explained by John in his description of Jesus' ministry. His book begins by asserting that the Word, the creative activity of God through all eternity, was made flesh in the person of Jesus. His own people did not accept him, but to everyone who did accept him he gave the right to become a child of God. The Law was given through Moses, but grace and truth came through Jesus Christ.

In several passages John writes about Jesus' claims about himself. For example, one evening Nicodemus, a leading Pharisee, visited him. He told Jesus that he believed him to be a teacher sent by God. Jesus responded by saying that only those who are born again through water and the Spirit can see the kingdom of God. "How is that possible?" asked Nicodemus. Jesus rebuked him, a Jewish teacher, for his inability to understand the truth. Then he claimed a special relationship with, and a special mission from, God. He said: "God loved the world so much that he sent his only Son, so that everyone who has faith in him should not perish but have eternal life. God did not send his Son to judge the world, but to save it."

On another occasion Jesus engaged in conversation with a Samaritan woman who came to draw water at a well. She was astonished when Jesus asked her for a drink, because there was deep hostility between Jews and Samaritans. But Jesus said: "If you only understood the gifts of God, and who is asking you for a drink, you would have asked him, and he would have given you living water. Everyone who drinks ordinary water will be thirsty again, but whoever drinks the water I offer will never be thirsty. The water I give will be a spring giving eternal life."

At first the woman misunderstood what was being said to her, and Jesus had to clear away misconceptions arising from her own sinfulness and from the controversies dividing Samaritans from Jews. Then he told her that he was in fact the Messiah. The woman told the people of her village what Jesus had said. He stayed there for two days and many of them became convinced that he was the Savior of the world.

John 1.1–18, 3.1–21, 4.1–42

34 ON THE WAY TO JERUSALEM

The time came for Jesus to make his final visit to Jerusalem. On the way he continued to warn his disciples of the fate that awaited him, but they continued to fail to understand him, even though they saw him being fiercely critical of the Jewish leadership and protective of people whom most Jews despised. He accused the Pharisees, the strictest of all Jews in their observance, of hypocrisy. This was because, although the Pharisees kept the outward requirements of the Jewish Law rigorously, they disregarded its more profound requirements of justice and love. He claimed that the Pharisees and the teachers of the Law oppressed ordinary people and persecuted those who taught new religious truth, as he did.

On the journey Jesus constantly challenged the assumptions of those who heard him or offered him hospitality. Dining with a Pharisee, and seeing the competition among the guests for a place of honor, he used the occasion to teach that God will exalt the humble, and humble those who seek to be among the highest. He said hospitality should be offered, not to friends or well-off neighbors, but to those who are unable to return it. The host's reward would come when the righteous rose from the dead.

In another implied rebuke to his own people he told a story of guests refusing, with a variety of excuses, an invitation to a feast. In anger the host filled his house with the poor and maimed; there was no longer any room for those first invited.

As they were approaching the town of Jericho a blind beggar, using a form of address reserved for the Messiah, shouted out to him: "Jesus, Son of David, have pity on me." People told him to be quiet, but he continued shouting until Jesus sent for him and restored his sight.

When Jesus arrived in Jericho itself, a man named Zacchaeus, a wealthy tax-gatherer, climbed a tree in order to see him amidst the crowds. Observing him, Jesus invited himself to dinner at his house. During the meal Zacchaeus vowed to give half his possessions to the poor and to recompense everyone he had defrauded. Jesus rejoiced, saying: "Today salvation has come to this family. I have come to seek and to save those who are lost."

Luke 9.51, 11.37–52, 14.7–24, 18.31–19.10

35   ARRIVAL AT JERUSALEM

As Jesus and his disciples approached Jerusalem, James and John asked a favor: that, when Jesus came into his kingdom, they might sit on his right and his left. Jesus asked them if they were able to face what faced him; they said they were. Jesus told them that they would indeed suffer as he was going to, but that the highest places in his kingdom were not his to give. When the other disciples heard about this conversation they were indignant, so Jesus explained to them that any of his followers who wanted to be great must be prepared to serve as he was doing, giving his life as a ransom for others.

Just outside Jerusalem Jesus sent two of his disciples into a nearby village and told them to bring back a donkey that they would find tethered there. If they were challenged they were to say: "The Master needs it." They did as they had been told, and, when they had brought the donkey, they spread their cloaks on it. Other followers spread their garments and greenery from the fields on the road in front of Jesus, and as he rode into Jerusalem crowds acclaimed him, waving palm branches and shouting: "Praise God! God bless him who comes in the name of the Lord! God bless the kingdom of our father King David which is to come!" So a prophecy of Zechariah was fulfilled.

The next day Jesus went into the Temple and drove out those who bought and sold there. He declared that the Temple should be a house of prayer but that it had been turned into a den of thieves. The authorities wanted to arrest him, but they were frightened of the crowds who gathered around him and who were spellbound by his teaching.

One evening Jesus was eating in a friend's house in Bethany where he was staying. A woman came in with a jar of costly perfume and anointed him with it. Some of the guests were indignant, saying that the perfume could have been sold and the money given to the poor. But Jesus defended the woman, saying: "You can help the poor at any time, but, by anointing me, this woman has prepared my body for burial."

After this Judas Iscariot went to the Jewish authorities and offered to hand Jesus over to them. He was promised thirty pieces of silver to betray him. He began to plan how an arrest could be contrived.

Mark 10.32–45, 11.1–12, 15–19, 14.1–11;
John 12.13; Matthew 21.5, 26.14–16

36   JESUS TEACHES IN THE TEMPLE

As the festival of Passover approached, Jesus went daily to the Temple, and taught believers, the skeptical, and the hostile. One day he told a parable about a man who planted a vineyard and rented it out to tenants. When he sent servants to collect his share of the harvest, the tenants ill-treated them, beating some and killing others. Finally the owner sent his son in the hope that he, at least, would be treated with respect. The tenants, recognizing him as the heir and wishing to take the vineyard for themselves, killed him too. "How would the owner react?" Jesus asked his hearers. "By killing the tenants and giving the vineyard to others."

The Jewish leaders realized that this story was aimed at them—they were the tenants in the story. They would have liked to arrest Jesus, but they were frightened of the crowd's reaction. Instead they sent questioners to trap him into indiscretion. He was asked whether it was right to pay taxes to the Roman Emperor or not. Jesus asked to see a silver coin and enquired whose image was upon it. To the reply: "The Emperor's," he rejoined: "Give to the Emperor what is the Emperor's and to God what is God's."

A group of leading Jews, the Sadducees, did not believe in the resurrection of the dead, so some of them told Jesus a story about a woman who, in order to fulfill the requirements of the Jewish law, married seven brothers in succession, in the vain hope of producing an heir. "To which of them," they asked, "would she be married when the dead rise?" Jesus replied: "There is no marriage after the resurrection of the dead; but how can you deny that the dead will rise? The God of Abraham and Isaac and Jacob is the God of the living, not of the dead."

Asked what the foremost commandment was, Jesus replied that there were two greater than all the others. The first is "Hear, O Israel, the Lord our God is one Lord, and you must love the Lord your God with all your heart, with all your soul, with all your mind and with all your strength." The second is: "You must love your neighbor as yourself."

Mark 11.27–12.34

37 TEACHING ABOUT JUDGMENT

During the last weeks of his ministry, Jesus spoke at length about difficult times to come and about the necessity of being prepared for God's judgment.

When his disciples admired the Temple building, he prophesied that it would be destroyed. He taught that times of human and natural disaster were coming; that his followers would be brought before courts and be beaten and executed; and that, in the face of danger, the only recourse would be to instant flight. During the times of turmoil there would be many false prophets and Messiahs, but finally the Son of Man—he himself—would appear to gather to himself those who had been faithful to him. Only God knew when this event would occur, and so Jesus' followers must be constantly ready and constantly on the watch.

To illustrate this teaching, he told a parable about a man going abroad and entrusting three of his servants with portions of his capital. On his return he summoned them to give account of themselves. Two of the servants had doubled their investments; he gave them extra responsibility and admitted them to his high favor. The servant to whom he had entrusted the least had done least with it; he simply returned the original sum he had been given. This dereliction of duty angered his master; he gave the investment to the servant who had earned most, and dismissed the idle one from his service. Jesus concluded: "Everyone who has will be given much more; but he who has not will be deprived of even the little he possesses."

In another parable Jesus described the Son of Man coming with his angels, sitting on the throne of judgment, and dividing humanity into two groups, the sheep and the goats. He set the sheep on his right and the goats on his left. He said to those on his right: "Come, enter into God's kingdom. You fed me when I was hungry, gave me drink, hospitality, and clothing when I was in need, and visited me when I was sick and in prison." Those to whom he spoke were surprised, and asked him when they had helped him. The Son of Man replied: "Whatever you did to help anyone, however insignificant, you did for me." But to those on his left he said: "Because you have failed to help those in need, you have failed to help me." They were sent away to eternal punishment, while the righteous entered eternal life.

Mark 13; Matthew 25.14–46

On the day before he died, Jesus ate with his disciples in the upper room of a house in Jerusalem. During the meal he blessed and broke bread, gave it to his disciples, and said: "This is my body given for you. Do this in memory of me." After supper he shared a cup of wine with them, saying: "This cup, poured out for you, is the new covenant sealed by my blood. Whenever you drink it, do this in memory of me."

Jesus then warned Peter that he would undergo a time of trial. In reply Peter exclaimed: "Lord, I am willing to go to prison and to death with you!" Jesus replied: "You will deny me three times before the cock crows tomorrow."

During the meal he washed the feet of his disciples, a duty usually undertaken by a slave. He told them that if he, their teacher and Lord, was prepared to serve them they ought to be prepared to serve each other in the same way. Then, in great distress, he said that one of the disciples was going to betray him. Later Judas left the meal for that very purpose, without the other disciples realizing what his intention was.

After Judas had left, Jesus spoke at length with the eleven, preparing them for what lay ahead. In earlier teaching he had called himself the bread of life, the light of the world, the good shepherd, and the resurrection and the life. Now he told them that he was the way, the truth, and the life and that the way to God the Father lay through him. He described himself as the true vine; only branches that remain united with the vine can bear fruit. Commanding them to love each other as he had loved them, he said that the highest expression of love was to lay down one's life for one's friends. He warned them to expect hatred and persecution, but promised them the gift of the Holy Spirit, who would enable them to remember what they had been taught and who would guide them into further truth. Finally he prayed for those whom God had called out of the world into union with himself. He asked that they might share his joy and glory, and be one in him.

Luke 22.1–20; 1 Corinthians 11.24–25; John 13–17

39   THE GARDEN OF GETHSEMANE

After leaving the upper room, Jesus led his disciples to the Mount of Olives just outside Jerusalem. When they reached a place called Gethsemane he took Peter, James, and John, and went apart from the other disciples to pray. In great distress he said to the three disciples: "My heart is breaking with grief; stay here and watch with me." Going a little further away, he threw himself to the ground and prayed that he might be spared what was to come. His prayer was: "Father, everything is possible for you; take this cup from me. Yet not my will but yours be done."

Returning to his friends he found them asleep. He urged them to stay awake and to pray that they might be delivered from temptation. Nonetheless they fell asleep twice more. As he roused them for the third time, an armed crowd, sent by the Jewish authorities and guided by Judas, arrived.

Judas had told those with him: "Arrest the man whom I kiss, and lead him away." Going up to Jesus he said "Rabbi!" and kissed him. Those with Judas seized Jesus, and there was a brief struggle during which one of the high priest's servants lost an ear. Jesus touched and healed him, and asked: "Do you think I am a robber, that you come to arrest me with swords and cudgels? I taught in the

Temple daily and you left me alone there. However, let the Scriptures be fulfilled." Then all his disciples deserted him and ran away.

After his arrest Jesus was taken to the house of the high priest Caiaphas. Peter followed at a distance, and joined a group sitting by a fire in the courtyard. A serving maid stared at him and said: "This man was with them." Peter replied: "I do not know him." As the night wore on, two other people accused him of being a companion of Jesus, one of them pointing out that his accent indicated that he came from Galilee, but each time he denied it strongly. Just after his third denial the cock crowed. Jesus turned and looked at Peter, who remembered Jesus' prophecy and his own pledge of the previous evening. He went outside and wept bitterly.

Mark 14.26–50; Luke 22.51–62

During the night Jesus' guards insulted and tormented him. They blindfolded and beat him, saying mockingly: "If you are a prophet, tell us who hit you." When morning came Jesus was brought before the Jewish Governing Council, which consisted of the chief priests, elders, and teachers of the Law. "Tell us," they said, "if you are the Messiah, the Son of God." His reply, "It is you who say that I am," was regarded as sufficient evidence for his condemnation for blasphemy. He was taken before Pontius Pilate, the Roman governor, and accused of claiming to be King of the Jews and thus of subverting Roman rule. After interrogating him Pilate concluded he had done nothing wrong, and was inclined to release him. When, however, he discovered that Jesus came from Galilee, he sent him to be judged by the ruler of that province, Herod son of Herod the Great, who happened to be in Jerusalem.

Herod had heard a great deal about Jesus and had long wanted to meet him. He questioned him at length, but Jesus refused to reply. Eventually Herod sent him back to Pilate arrayed in a gorgeous robe, thereby making up a quarrel between them.

Pilate still believed that Jesus was being falsely accused, and his wife sent him a message to the same effect. So he decided to take advantage of a custom by which a prisoner chosen by the people was released at Passover-tide. He was holding another well-known prisoner whose name was Jesus Barabbas, and he asked the crowd that had gathered: "Which one would you like me to release—Jesus Barabbas or Jesus who is called the Messiah?" The chief priests and elders had worked on the crowd, so they responded "Barabbas." "What then am I to do with Jesus called Messiah?" asked Pilate. The reply came repeatedly and with increasing emphasis: "Crucify him!"

When Pilate saw that his efforts to save Jesus were fruitless, and that there was a danger of a riot breaking out, he took water and washed his hands, saying; "My hands are clean of this man's blood." He released Barabbas and had Jesus flogged; then he handed him over to be crucified. The soldiers made sport of him, stripping him, dressing him in a scarlet cloak, and putting a reed in his hand and a crown of thorns on his head. They paid him mock homage, spat upon him, and beat him. Then they put on his clothes again, and led him away.

Luke 22.63–23.12; Matthew 27.15–31

41 THE CRUCIFIXION

By then Jesus was too weak to carry his cross to the place of execution, so the soldiers compelled a man named Simon from Cyrene in North Africa to carry it for him. Among the great crowd that followed him were many women, who wept for him. Jesus told them to weep for themselves and for their children because dreadful times were coming.

When they reached the place called "The Skull" the soldiers crucified him and two criminals, one of them on his right and one on his left. Jesus said: "Father, forgive them; they do not know what they are doing." Above his head was an inscription saying "The King of the Jews." The soldiers shared out his clothes by casting lots; they and the crowd, which included Jewish leaders, jeered at him, saying: "He saved other people; now let him save himself if he really is God's chosen Messiah." Even one of the criminals crucified with him joined in the taunting, but the other reproached him, saying: "We are getting what we deserve, but this man has done nothing wrong." Then he said to Jesus: "Remember me when you inherit your kingdom." Jesus replied: "Today you will be with me in Paradise."

From midday darkness fell until three o'clock in the afternoon. Then Jesus shouted: "My God, my

God, why have you deserted me?" Some of the bystanders thought he was calling upon Elijah; one of them offered him wine in a sponge held on the end of a stick, and said: "Let's see if Elijah will come and help him." Jesus then gave another loud cry and died; and at that very moment the curtain dividing the Holy of Holies from the rest of the Temple building was torn in two. When the Roman officer who had supervised the execution saw how Jesus had died he said: "This man was really God's Son."

The day was a Friday, the eve of the Sabbath, and the Jews were anxious that the bodies should not remain on the crosses once the Sabbath had begun. Pilate therefore agreed that the legs of the condemned men should be broken, to hasten their deaths. This was done in the cases of the two criminals, but when the soldiers came to Jesus they found he was already dead. They did not break his legs, but one of them thrust a spear into his side, causing a flow of blood and water.

Luke 23.26–43; Mark 15.33–39;
John 19.31–37

42   JESUS RISES FROM THE DEAD

That Friday evening Joseph of Arimathea, a member of the Jewish Governing Council but also a follower of Jesus, asked Pilate if he might have Jesus' body. Once Pilate had given permission, the body was taken down from the cross and wrapped in a linen sheet. Then it was laid in a tomb cut out of the rock, which Joseph had prepared for himself, and a large stone was rolled in front of it. Some of the women who had witnessed the crucifixion watched over the grave.

The next day the Jewish leaders asked Pilate if they could protect the tomb with a guard, lest the disciples should come, steal the body, and then falsely claim that Jesus had risen from the dead. Pilate agreed to their request, and the tomb was sealed and guarded.

At daybreak on Sunday, two days later, Mary Magdalene and another Mary, two of the women who had watched over the tomb, visited it again. Suddenly there was a violent earthquake and an angel, descending from heaven, rolled away the stone in front of the tomb, and sat upon it. He said to the women: "Do not be afraid. Jesus has been raised and is going before you to Galilee. Go quickly, and tell his disciples."

As the women hurried away in awe and joy, they were met by Jesus himself. They knelt before him; he told them to continue with their errand and to deliver the message the angel had given them. Meanwhile the guards at the tomb, who had been overcome with fear when the angel appeared, returned to the Jewish leaders and told them what had happened. The leaders bribed them to say that the disciples had come by night and stolen the body, and this story was circulated widely.

Later that day two downcast followers of Jesus were walking to the village of Emmaus, seven miles from Jerusalem. Jesus joined them on the road, but they did not recognize him. He asked the reason for their sadness, and they told him of all that had recently occurred in Jerusalem. In response he used the Scriptures to explain that it was necessary for the Messiah to suffer before being glorified. When the travelers reached their home they invited him in, and, as he blessed and broke bread, they realized who he was. Then he disappeared, and they immediately set off back to Jerusalem to tell the other disciples what they had seen and heard.

Matthew 27.37–28.15; Luke 24.13–33

43   FURTHER RESURRECTION
APPEARANCES

When the pair from Emmaus reached Jerusalem they shared their experiences with the disciples there, who told them that Peter too had seen Jesus. As they were talking Jesus appeared, greeting them with the words "Peace be with you." At first they were all terrified, and thought they were seeing a ghost; but he said: "Why are you worried and doubtful? Look at my hands and feet and touch me; no ghost has flesh and bones as I do." He further convinced them by eating a piece of fish. He explained once again how the Scriptures had foretold his sufferings and resurrection, and said that repentance and the forgiveness of sins were to be preached in his name to the whole world. Then he led them to Bethany, blessed them, and was parted from them. Full of joy, they returned to Jerusalem and praised God daily in the Temple.

One of the apostles, Thomas the twin, had not been with the others that day, and refused to believe in the resurrection without physical proof. A week later Jesus appeared to the disciples again, and invited Thomas to touch the wounds in his hands and his side. Thomas exclaimed: "My Lord and my God!" Jesus said to him: "Because you have seen me you have found faith. Happy are they who find faith without seeing me."

Some time later a group of disciples, led by Peter, returned to Galilee and spent a fruitless night fishing. When dawn came Jesus was standing at the water's edge. He called to them to make a further cast of the net, and when they did so, they made so large a catch that they could not haul the net into the boat. Realizing that it was Jesus who had hailed them, Peter plunged into the water to reach him while the others brought the boat ashore.

The disciples breakfasted on food that Jesus had prepared; then he took Peter aside, and three times asked him "Do you love me?" Three times Peter replied that he did, and three times Jesus told him: "Tend my sheep." Then he promised him a martyr's death.

Jesus did much else that has not been recorded here. These stories have been told in order that you might believe that Jesus is the Son of God, and that through faith in him you may have eternal life.

Luke 24.33–53; John 20.24–21.19

44   THE ASCENSION, PENTECOST, AND THE EARLY CHURCH

The risen Jesus appeared to his friends over forty days. A final meeting took place on the Mount of Olives near Jerusalem; there, having promised them the gift of the Holy Spirit and having commanded them to bear witness to him to the ends of the earth, he ascended into heaven.

During the Jewish feast of Pentecost, which came soon afterward, the Holy Spirit descended on them in wind and flame, and inspired them to speak in other tongues. People from all over the Mediterranean world who were in Jerusalem during the festival were astonished when they heard them. Peter told the crowd that the prophet Joel had foretold this outpouring of the Holy Spirit, and that Jesus, whom they had crucified, had risen from the dead as Lord and Christ.

Many of Peter's audience joined the infant Christian Church, which grew to be several thousand strong. They shared their possessions and worshipped both in the Temple and in their homes. They soon attracted the attention of the authorities, but their leaders defied injunctions not to speak about Jesus. Warnings gave way to threats and then to floggings, but the Church continued to grow.

The Church appointed seven officers called deacons to look after their poorest members. The preaching of one of them, Stephen, aroused bitter hostility, and he was brought before the Jewish authorities. Replying to the charges against him, he showed how Jesus fit into the sacred history of the Jews, and accused them of constantly rejecting those whom God had sent them. When he claimed to see Jesus standing at God's right hand, he was stoned to death.

A young man called Saul, a devout Pharisee from the city of Tarsus in Asia Minor, joined enthusiastically in the persecution of Christians. He was sent to Damascus with letters authorizing him to arrest any Christians he found there. On his journey a light from heaven flashed around him and he fell to the ground. A voice said: "Saul, why are you persecuting me?" Saul said: "Lord, who are you?" The voice replied: "I am Jesus. Go into the city and you will be told what to do." When the vision passed Saul found he was blind, and so his companions led him into Damascus. There a Christian named Ananias was told in a vision to visit him. He did so, cured his blindness, and conferred the Holy Spirit on him. Saul was baptized, and immediately began to teach that Jesus was the Son of God.

Acts 1.1–9.22

45 THE CHRISTIAN CHURCH GROWS AND DEVELOPS

In ensuing years Christian congregations were set up throughout the eastern Mediterranean. It soon became a burning issue whether Gentiles (non-Jews) could become Christians without becoming Jews as well.

On a missionary tour around some of the new congregations, Peter came to Joppa. There he had a vision in which a sheet containing creatures of every description, including those that Jews were forbidden to eat, was lowered from heaven. A voice commanded: "Get up, Peter, kill and eat." Peter refused, saying he had never eaten anything unclean. The response came: "It is not for you to call unclean anything which God calls clean." While Peter was puzzling over this experience, a messenger summoned him to Caesarea, where a devout Roman centurion called Cornelius asked him to speak about his faith. As Peter did so the Holy Spirit descended upon his hearers, all Gentiles. Because of his vision Peter had no hesitation in baptizing them.

Meanwhile Saul, now generally known by his Roman name of Paul, based himself in the town of Antioch in Cilicia, and from there undertook missionary journeys to neighboring lands. His standard practice was to preach first in the local synagogue, to Jews and people who were not Jews but who attended Jewish worship; then, if his ministry was rejected, he left the synagogue and preached only to Gentiles. He was much harassed by those Jews whom he failed to convert; he had to flee from place to place, and on one occasion was stoned and left for dead. Meanwhile the persecution of Christians continued elsewhere. Herod beheaded James the brother of John, and imprisoned Peter, who was preserved only by a miraculous escape from prison.

The admission of Gentiles to the Church remained a contentious topic, and a council was held in Jerusalem to decide what policy should be. The conclusion was that it was not necessary for Christians from a Gentile background to keep the Jewish Law, save in certain minor respects. This decision opened the way for the Church to spread more rapidly still.

On another missionary journey Paul crossed over to the European mainland and evangelized in Greece. In Philippi in Macedonia he and his companion were flogged and imprisoned after Paul had cured a possessed slave girl. They refused the opportunity to escape that an earthquake afforded, and so impressed the prison governor that he and all his family were baptized.

Acts 9.31–16.40

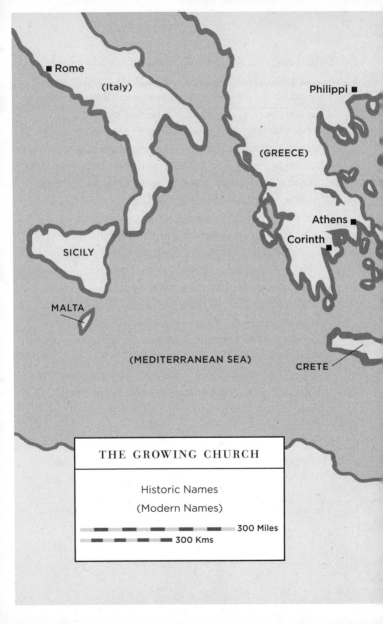

Rome

(Italy)

Philippi

(GREECE)

Athens

Corinth

SICILY

MALTA

(MEDITERRANEAN SEA)

CRETE

THE GROWING CHURCH

Historic Names

(Modern Names)

300 Miles

300 Kms

46 FURTHER EXPANSION: PAUL'S TRAVELS

Paul traveled on through Greece, gaining converts and provoking opposition wherever he went. In Athens he was greeted with lively curiosity but made only a few converts. In Corinth the local Jews brought him before the Roman governor Gallio, but Gallio refused to intervene in what he considered to be a dispute within the Jewish community.

Later Paul came to Ephesus in Asia Minor. His successful ministry there enraged the local silversmiths, whose living came from making statues of the city's deity, Artemis. A serious riot broke out; Paul wanted to speak to the protesters, but, fearing for his safety, the local Christians would not allow it. It was left to a local official to quell the crowd and restore order.

In due course Paul decided to return to Jerusalem, even though he knew that he was putting himself in grave danger; on his way he visited churches that he had established earlier, to say good-bye. In Jerusalem he visited James, the brother of Jesus and head of the church there, and was asked to prove that he still thought of himself as a Jew by undertaking a ritual purification in the Temple. While he was doing so he was recognized and accused of profaning the Jewish faith and the Temple itself. He was rescued from the fury of the mob by a detachment from the Roman garrison, and subsequently from a plot to murder him by being taken to Caesarea. There he was brought before two successive Roman governors, the second of whom asked him to return to Jerusalem and stand trial before a Jewish court. To have agreed would have meant certain death, so Paul took advantage of the fact that he had been born a Roman citizen, and appealed to the Emperor. This meant that he would have to travel as a prisoner to Rome.

The ship on which he and his companions were embarked set sail for Rome, but was caught in a storm and wrecked on the coast of Malta. Thanks to Paul's leadership, the crew and passengers all came safely ashore; it was only after some months that he set sail again and came to Rome. He was greeted warmly by the Christians there, and imprisoned in comfortable circumstances to await his trial. Once again most of the local Jews rejected his teaching, and once again he turned to the Gentiles, teaching them without hindrance.

Acts 17–28

47   THE YOUNG CHURCH: DOCTRINE

The letters written to congregations and individuals by early Christian leaders guided people in the way of Christ. Paul taught that, ever since the days of Adam, humankind has been inherently sinful. God gave his chosen people, the Jews, the Law as guidance for behavior and so that sinfulness should become apparent. But a right relationship with God depends not on trying to keep the Law, but on faith in the saving death of Jesus Christ. Jesus was in the form of God, but for our sake he laid aside his divine attributes and became a humble human being. He lived a life of obedience to the divine will, to the point of dying on the cross. Then he was raised and exalted, and now he reigns in heaven as Lord.

Through Jesus' self-giving love, reconciliation between humankind and God has become possible. All those who have faith and been baptized have received the Holy Spirit, and have entered into a new life, shared with and depending upon the life of Christ. Christians must still wrestle with their old sinful nature; but they can be confident that in the strength of the Holy Spirit they will gradually be transformed into the new people God wishes them to be. After death comes resurrection, when our human, perishable bodies will give place to bodies that are imperishable and immortal.

The Holy Spirit confers gifts on individual Christians. For example, they may be able to teach, to administer, to heal, or to speak in tongues. Each gift enables its recipient to play a part in the Church, which is the body of Christ, continuing his work on earth. The Spirit also bears fruit in individual lives, producing such virtues as love, joy, peace, patience, kindness, goodness, fidelity, gentleness, and self-control.

The greatest gift is love. Love is patient and kind; envies no one, and is neither boastful nor conceited; is never rude, selfish, or quick to take offense. Love does not count up grievances or take pleasure in the failings of others. Love's joy is in the truth: there is no limit to its faith, hope, and endurance.

The letter to the Hebrews explains Jesus' significance in another way, using a metaphor based on the Jewish sacrificial system. Jesus is the great high priest, entering the Holy of Holies to offer the perfect sacrifice of himself. The old sacrifices could not take away sin and needed constant repetition, but Christ's sacrifice takes away sin once and for all.

Romans; 1 Corinthians; Galatians; Philippians; Hebrews

48 THE YOUNG CHURCH: DIFFICULTIES

As Christianity spread, and as non-Jews joined the church in large numbers, many problems arose. Paul addressed some of them in his letters.

In Corinth the church had divided into parties, each claiming a prominent Christian as its leader. Paul pointed out that the Church had only one true leader—Christ—and that unity in Christ was essential. So was mutual respect. Christians were variously gifted, but no one gift was more important than another. All were essential for building up the Church, the body of Christ.

There were sometimes questions about finance. While Paul paid his own way, he thought that apostles had a right to support from the churches they served. He also thought local churches should look beyond themselves to the needs of others. He organized a collection on behalf of the church in Jerusalem, which had fallen upon hard times, and encouraged churches far and wide to contribute to it.

Paul believed that the Christian community should resolve disagreements among its members without resorting to the secular courts. Those guilty of sexual immorality should be disciplined. While celibacy was admirable, it was not for everybody. Marriage, through which a man and a woman became one flesh, was the only right way of expressing sexuality physically. Marriage should be permanent; it was only when a believing and an unbelieving partner could not agree to live together that separation should occur.

It was difficult for Christians to decide how far they should separate themselves from the practices of their pagan neighbors when they spilled over into daily life. Paul's advice was that there was nothing intrinsically wrong in, for example, eating meat that had been offered to an idol, but the first priority was to do nothing that might hurt other Christians who thought differently.

The religious meals of the Corinthian church, held, as were all early meetings for worship, in private houses, had degenerated because the food families brought had not been shared, and the poor had been left hungry. Paul taught that the Lord's Supper should be a communal meal, and that the act of worship should derive from the words of Jesus at the Last Supper. Worship should not be dominated by speaking in tongues, but should also include prayer, prophecy, and hymn-singing, with leadership widely shared among the men present.

1 and 2 Corinthians

49 THE YOUNG CHURCH: DAILY LIFE

The letters written by Paul and others contain much practical advice about how Christians, living in a world that was often uncomprehending and hostile, should conduct themselves in daily life.

They were to abstain from foolish and damaging speech; from drunkenness and dissipation; from coarse and flippant talk; from envy and contention; from anger and selfish ambition; from greed and from retaliation for harm done to them; from sexual relations outside marriage. They were to be patient under persecution. The wealthy among them were to remember the impermanence of riches, to repent of their misuse, and to be generous in well-doing. They were to fill their minds with thoughts that were true, noble, just, pure, loving, attractive, excellent, and admirable.

Christians were to regard every other Christian, no matter what his or her status or background, as a brother or sister, equally entitled to respect, love, and care in times of need. They were to be tolerant of disagreements about religious practice. They were to be peaceable citizens, praying for their rulers and being obedient to authority. Men should love their wives in the same way that Christ loves his Church, and treat their children and their slaves with justice and kindness. Wives should be obedient to their husbands and modest in their appearance and behavior; children and slaves should be obedient and diligent. Generous hospitality was a duty.

Paul illustrated the Christian life in action in a letter to his Christian friend Philemon. One of Philemon's slaves, Onesimus, had run away, had met Paul, and had become a Christian. Paul sent him back to Philemon, asking him to forgive Onesimus' offenses and to receive him as a brother.

Above all, the Christian life should be infused with love. Christians should love each other because God is love. God showed his love by sending his Son as a sacrifice for our sins, in order to give us eternal life. Christians know that they live in him and he in them because he has given his Holy Spirit to them. The gift and the seal of the Spirit is love; anyone who lives in love lives in God, and God lives in him. Love does away with the fear of judgment; but anyone who claims to love God while hating a fellow Christian is deceiving himself. Whoever loves God must love his fellow Christians too.

Romans; Ephesians; Philippians; 1 Timothy; James; 1 Peter; Philemon; 1 John

50   REVELATION

A Christian named John, in exile on the Mediterranean island of Patmos, wrote about a series of visions granted to him. He saw the risen Jesus, and was entrusted by him with messages to seven churches in Asia Minor. The messages comforted the churches in their affliction and praised them for their virtues, but they also contained sharp criticisms of respects in which they had fallen short. For example, the church at Laodicea was criticized for being lukewarm in its devotion and complacent in its prosperity. The message went on: "Behold, I stand knocking at your door. If anyone opens the door I will come in and he and I will eat together."

John's visions turned to the heavenly court where God the Father sat enthroned in glory and honor, surrounded by creatures both human and not, and receiving unending hymns of praise. With him stood the Lamb (that is, Jesus) who, by opening a scroll, loosed dreadful disasters on the earth; only the true servants of God were exempt, with special honor being accorded to those who had died as martyrs. Further visions of judgment followed, culminating in a prophecy that Rome, the great Babylon, would be utterly destroyed. All this was part of a cosmic struggle between the forces of good and evil, which ended with the Devil being defeated and cast into an everlasting lake of fire. All humankind was judged, and those whose names were not found in the book of life were cast into the lake of fire too.

Then a new heaven and a new earth emerged. The Holy City, a new Jerusalem, came down from heaven. It needed no temple because God was fully present there; nor did it need the sun or moon because of the divine light that pervaded it. Through the city flowed the river of the water of life; and within it God's servants saw him and the Lamb face to face forever.

The visions ended with Jesus saying: "Let the thirsty come; let whoever so desires receive the water of life. Yes, I am coming soon"; and John responding: "Amen! Come, Lord Jesus."

Revelation